By Adryan Moorefield
Conceived By Adryan Moorefield & TJ Perry
Illustrated By Naira Tangamyan

Hey There Little Black Girl

59 Affirmations To Help You Learn Your Feelings

AuthorHouse™
1663 Liberty Drive
Bloomington, IN 47403
www.authorhouse.com
Phone: 833-262-8899

Because of the dynamic nature of the Internet, any web addresses or links contained in this book may have changed since
publication and may no longer be valid. The views expressed in this work are solely those of the author and do not necessarily
reflect the views of the publisher, and the publisher hereby disclaims any responsibility for them.

Any people depicted in stock imagery provided by Getty Images are models,
and such images are being used for illustrative purposes only.
Certain stock imagery © Getty Images.

This book is printed on acid-free paper.

ISBN: 978-1-6655-4367-5 (sc)
978-1-6655-4368-2 (e)

Published by AuthorHouse 11/05/2021

Library of Congress Control Number: 2021923145

Rev. Date: 11/11/2021

authorHOUSE®

How to Read This Book

This book is a guide to help you learn your feelings.
Whenever you feel a certain emotion, go to that section in this book.
Take a deep breath and pick a page.
Pick a sentence on the page and let that sink in.
Lather, rinse, and repeat as often as you need to.
Use this book throughout the day whenever you feel overwhelmed by your emotions.
Before long, you will be equipped with the tools you need
to be a confident, well rounded, centered human being.

Appearance

Hey there little black girl,
love the skin you're in.
You are wrapped in kisses from the sun.
That glow will always win!

Hello there little black girl,
your hair is beautiful
and strong.
It holds stories from
your ancestors.
Those tales are
never wrong!

Hey there little black girl,
your shape is
one of a kind.
Be healthy, live strong,
have fun,
and laugh. What counts
is in your mind!

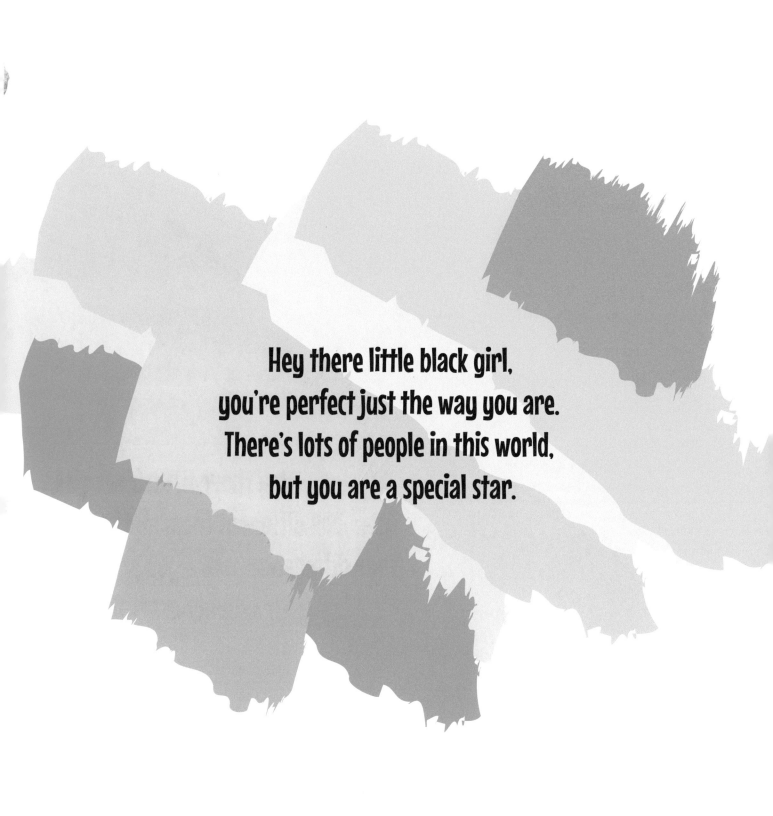

Hey there little black girl,
you're perfect just the way you are.
There's lots of people in this world,
but you are a special star.

Hey there little black girl, that reflection you see is light. Don't be afraid to let it shine, for yours is really bright!

Hey there little black girl, you look different from all the rest. Your differences make you powerful, your uniqueness is the best.

Hey there little black girl, your eyes are a gorgeous shade. They carry treasure no one else knows, your eyes are wondrously made.

Hey there little black girl,
your lips are the perfect size.
They help you speak with authority,
from them will come no lies!

Hey there little black girl,
your teeth are just right!
Your smile can brighten any
room, just brush
to keep them white.

Hey there little black girl,
you are beautiful, yes indeed.
You are a gift given to the world.
Your gift is what we need!

Happy

Hey there little black girl,
your smile is beautiful
and bright!
It shines as strong as
one thousand suns.
It can light up any night!

Hey there little black girl,
you're feeling really good today.
Use that feeling, be kind and helpful,
your generosity goes a long way.

Hey there little black girl, I've got a challenge for you. Do something nice for someone else today, then they'll be happy too!

Hey there little black girl, it feels so good to play. Your laughter is contagious. You will liven any day!

Hey there little black girl,
find joy in any place.
That power will cover your entire being,
it will keep a smile on your face.

Hey there little black girl,
go on and explore.
Your passions will
propel you, they
can open any door.

Hey there little black girl,
I watch you sing and dance.
Your energy is enchanting.
You've put me in a trance.

Hey there little black girl,
I want to make a deal.
Be kind to others,
don't pick and choose.
Care about how
they feel.

Hey there little black girl,
go ahead and touch the sky.
No dream is impossible.
No mountain is too high!

Hey there little black girl,
you're not like
anyone I've seen.
You descend from
royalty! Remember
you are a QUEEN!

Sad

Hey there little black girl,
I see you're sad today!
It's ok to feel the way you feel,
something better could be
coming your way.

Hey there little black girl,
your tears are
really wet.
It's ok to cry,
or talk things out,
you'll soon
feel better yet!

Hey there little black girl, your feelings really matter. Don't let anyone tell you otherwise, ignore all that chatter!

Hey there little black girl, you seem to be in pain. That feeling will eventually disappear. You'll soon feel good again.

Hey there little black girl,
you won't always be the best.
Don't let the ranks define you,
there isn't any test!

Hey there little black girl,
sometimes things
will be lost.
Memories are priceless,
they don't
have any cost.

Hey there little black girl, goodbyes can cause
some strife. Honor the time you
had together, that
growth is a way of life.

Hey there little black girl,
you are a special cup of tea.
Not everyone will like it but
that leaves more room just for me!

Hey there little black girl,
things just aren't going your way.
Everyone has bad luck sometimes,
tomorrow's another day.

Hey there little black girl,
friendships come and go.
Just give it time,
you'll find
your tribe, these friends
are Best in Show!

Angry

Hey there little black girl, I see you're really
mad. Take a moment, think things
through, I'm sure things
aren't that bad!

Hey there little black girl,
someone was really mean.
It doesn't feel good to not be
heard, all you want is to be seen!

Hey there little black girl, you're throwing
a big fit! There are better ways
to communicate,
but first you
have to quit!

Hey there little black girl,
it's hard when you
don't agree. Everyone has different
thoughts, you must accept this to be free.

Hey there little black girl,
respect you do deserve.
Don't let others put you down
but calm that
raging nerve!

Hey there little black girl,
your patience is running thin.
Take a step back and breathe real deep.
The right words will help you win.

Hey there
little black girl,
your head is
fuming with steam.
You'll have the urge to
act it out,
find a pillow
instead and scream!

Hey there little black girl,
sometimes it's hard to do the right thing.
Don't let your anger conquer you or
the consequences could sting!

Hey there little black girl,
life isn't always fair.
As frustrating as
that fact may be,
there's goodness in the air.

Scared

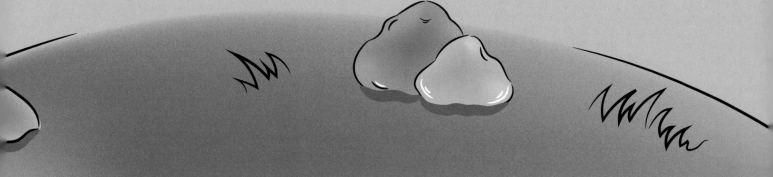

Hey there little black girl,
you're shaking in your bones.
Everyone is afraid of
something.
I promise you're
not alone!

Hey there little black girl, it's ok to cry.
That mountain might
look real big, you can
climb it if you try!

Hey there little black girl,
you're stronger than you know.
The first step is always
the hardest, all you have to do is go!

Hey there little black girl,
that job looks really tough.
Just give it your best,
that's all I ask.
Remember you
are enough!

Hey there little black girl, did something frighten you? Look your fear straight in the face and tell that fear to move!

Hey there little black girl, the unknown can be scary. Take a leap of faith, you've got this now. There's no need to stay wary.

Hey there little black girl,
you can do it if you try.
The thought of
failing can be
tough. Just spread
your wings and fly!

Hey there little black girl,
your fear can be a key.
It tells you when you should be careful,
that voice can help you see.

Hey there little black girl, when fear looks you
in the face, sometimes there's
strength in numbers.
All you need's a warm embrace.

Hey there little black girl,
you won't always be afraid.
With just a little courage,
your fear will start to fade.

Embarrassed

Hey there little black girl,
it seems you made a mistake.
Bloopers happen,
nobody's perfect.
If we were, we'd all be fake!

Hey there little black girl, that didn't go quite
as you thought. Your life isn't over,
you can try again,
mistakes will happen a lot!

Hey there little black girl,
put that feeling up on a shelf.
Say, "Hello, how are you?
I am human! Don't be so hard on yourself!"

Hey there little black girl,
your cheeks are
looking flush.
Whatever you did,
it will be ok,
let's take away that blush!

Hey there little black girl, did you just trip and fall?
Brush yourself off and dry
those eyes, your win
is waiting afterall.

Hey there little black girl,
bruises come and go.
Don't let that voice inside your
head take over, just say no!

Hey there little black girl, there's no need
to feel ashamed. Everyone has their
moments, for that
you can't be blamed.

Hey there little black girl,
your decision wasn't the best.
Next time you'll be ready.
You're sure to pass that test.

Hey there little black girl, this time the joke's on you. When all you hear is laughter, you should just laugh too!

Letter From the Author

I want to start out by saying thank you! Thank you for taking the time to read this book.
Thank you for bringing your beautiful child into the world.
Thank you for instilling love and support into your child's life.
This book is a passion project for me and really serves to meet a need that I have had even well into my adult life.

My parents loved us. I have a brother and a sister and we all received our parent's love in different ways.
Unfortunately, receiving love from a parent isn't always enough.
I have found that a huge portion of the love that I didn't receive was not the responsibility of my parents to give.
I grew up not knowing the full extent of the love that I should have been showing myself.
I didn't have anyone to teach me to love myself.
To tell me that I was special, and magical, and wonderful, and talented, and perfectly imperfect. In my adult life,
I want to be that voice for so many children. That's where this book comes in.

This book is supposed to be a guide for parents to connect with their children.
To help them learn their feelings and figure out how to deal with them.
This book speaks to the hearts and souls of both the children this book targets and the parents that will read
this book to their children. We are all deserving of the love and magic that lie inside of us.
My hope is that this book will pave the way for showing each of us how to learn and love ourselves.

Happy reading!

Printed in the United States
by Baker & Taylor Publisher Services